FINDING INSPIRATION

BY ABBY COLICH

YO-DWI-272

DISCARD

BLUE OWL
BOOKS

TIPS FOR CAREGIVERS

Social and emotional learning (SEL) helps children manage emotions, learn how to feel empathy, create and achieve goals, and make good decisions. Strong lessons and support in SEL will help children establish positive habits in communication, cooperation, and decision-making. By incorporating SEL in early reading, children will learn the importance of respect and encouragement when working with others.

BEFORE READING

Talk to the reader about inspiration and what it means. Discuss how working with others can help us find inspiration. Talk about what it means to come up with and share ideas.

Discuss: Think of a time you have worked in a group. How did you get started? How did you come up with ideas?

AFTER READING

Talk to the reader about the importance of cooperation, respect, and encouragement when coming up with ideas.

Discuss: How can you encourage others when you are coming up with new ideas for a project? What are some ways you can share your own ideas?

SEL GOAL

Children may have a difficult time bringing SEL concepts into group work. Talk to readers about the importance of mindfulness and empathy when working with others. Ask readers to think of a time working with others went well and a time it did not. What happened each time? What did they learn? Explain that group work goes more smoothly when people encourage and respect one another.

R0461442528

TABLE OF CONTENTS

CHAPTER 1
Getting Started 4

CHAPTER 2
Sharing Ideas 6

CHAPTER 3
Making Decisions 18

GOALS AND TOOLS
Grow with Goals 22
Writing Reflection 22
Glossary 23
To Learn More 23
Index 24

GETTING STARTED

Working in a group is not always easy. But it can be fun and **rewarding**. You get to listen to others' ideas. You get to share your own. You can **inspire** one another.

How do you start? First, make sure everyone understands the project. Ask any questions you have. Discuss when the project is due. Talk about what your **goals** are. Write them down.

CHAPTER 2

SHARING IDEAS

Next, you will need to come up with ideas. Let's say you and your group have to create a board game. What kind of game will you create? How will you **collaborate**?

One way to come up with ideas is to **brainstorm**. Share whatever ideas come to mind. The more ideas, the better! Have one or two people in your group write down the ideas. You may want to set a time limit.

idea

Mind mapping is one way to brainstorm. Write your topic in the middle of a piece of paper. Circle it. Draw branches from it for each idea.

Carly and her group are doing a project about spiders. She makes a branch for each idea they might include in their project.

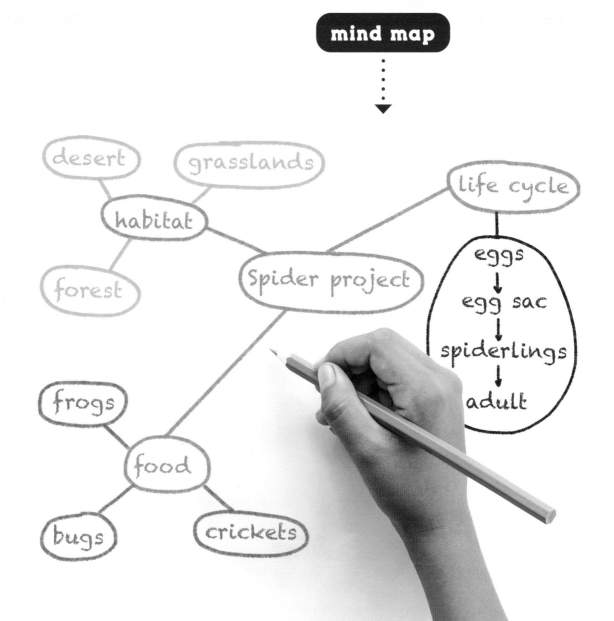

desert

grasslands

life cycle

habitat

Spider project

eggs
↓
egg sac
↓
spiderlings
↓
adult

forest

frogs

food

bugs

crickets

When you brainstorm, be **mindful**. Make sure everyone gets a chance to speak. **Encourage** others to share. If someone hasn't shared yet, try asking, "Did you have anything you wanted to say?" Or ask, "What do you think of this idea?"

ASK ONCE

Don't push people to speak in front of the group. They may be shy or uncomfortable. Ask once. Then move on if they don't feel like sharing.

Share your own ideas, even if you don't think they are your best. If you don't have any ideas, you can **contribute** by building others up. Say, "That's a great idea." Or you can add on to other ideas. Say, "I like what you said about including a chart. Maybe we can add that to our poster."

You may need to **research** to find inspiration. Use **sources**, such as books, websites, or videos.

Farah and her dance group are coming up with a new routine. They watch videos and listen to music for inspiration.

GIVE CREDIT

It is important to give **credit** if you get ideas or information from sources or other people. If you see an idea you like, be sure to note where it came from.

You may go somewhere or do something for inspiration. Tim and his group are working on a science project. They go outside to find ideas.

INSPIRING PLACES

Libraries and museums can be good places to visit to get ideas. If you can't go in person, visit the museum's website instead.

MAKING DECISIONS

When you have a list of ideas for your project, discuss them with your group. Every idea is important and should be considered. Maybe some ideas can be combined.

If people have different **preferences**, take a vote. Some people may need to **compromise**. Some might be upset their ideas weren't used. Show **empathy**. Say, "We liked your ideas. Maybe we can use them next time."

Remember that working together means putting everyone's ideas together to do your best work.

Keep sharing ideas, listening to everyone, and being respectful. With **teamwork**, you will do great things!

GOALS AND TOOLS

GROW WITH GOALS

Think about ways you can come up with ideas or help others come up with them.

Goal: Name some ways you can encourage others. What are some things you can say?

Goal: Try giving a compliment to someone whose idea you like. What could you say to that person?

Goal: Think about a time you were afraid to share an idea you had. What would you do differently now?

WRITING REFLECTION

Write about a time you had to compromise with someone. What happened? What did you have to give up? What did the other person have to give up? Were you happy with how things turned out? What might you do differently if you had another chance?

GLOSSARY

brainstorm
To come up with ideas or solutions to a problem.

collaborate
To work together to do something.

compromise
To agree to accept something that is not entirely what you wanted in order to satisfy some of the requests of other people.

contribute
To help in order to accomplish a specific goal.

credit
Recognition.

empathy
The ability to understand and be sensitive to the thoughts and feelings of others.

encourage
To give someone confidence, usually by using praise and support.

goals
Things you aim to do.

inspire
To influence and encourage someone to achieve or do something.

mindful
A mentality achieved by focusing on the present moment and calmly recognizing and accepting your feelings, thoughts, and sensations.

preferences
Things that people like or prefer over other things.

research
To collect information about something.

rewarding
Offering or bringing satisfaction.

sources
People, books, or documents that provide information.

teamwork
The work done by a group of people who accomplish something together.

TO LEARN MORE

FACT SURFER

Finding more information is as easy as 1, 2, 3.

1. Go to www.factsurfer.com

2. Enter "**findinginspiration**" into the search box.

3. Choose your book to see a list of websites.

INDEX

ask 5, 11

brainstorm 7, 8, 11

collaborate 6

compromise 19

discuss 5, 18

empathy 19

encourage 11

goals 5

libraries 16

listen 4, 15, 21

mindful 11

mind mapping 8

museums 16

questions 5

research 15

respectful 21

share 4, 7, 11, 12

sources 15

teamwork 21

topic 8

upset 19

vote 19

websites 15, 16

write 5, 7, 8

Blue Owl Books are published by Jump!, 5357 Penn Avenue South, Minneapolis, MN 55419, www.jumplibrary.com

Copyright © 2022 Jump! International copyright reserved in all countries. No part of this book may be reproduced in any form without written permission from the publisher.

Library of Congress Cataloging-in-Publication Data

Names: Colich, Abby, author.
Title: Finding inspiration / by Abby Colich.
Description: Minneapolis, MN: Jump!, Inc., [2022] | Series: Working together
Includes index. | Audience: Ages 7–10
Identifiers: LCCN 2020056039 (print)
LCCN 2020056040 (ebook)
ISBN 9781636901206 (hardcover)
ISBN 9781636901213 (paperback)
ISBN 9781636901220 (ebook)
Subjects: LCSH: Small groups–Juvenile literature. | Brainstorming–Juvenile literature.
Group decision making–Juvenile literature. | Social skills in children–Juvenile literature.
Classification: LCC HM736 .C65 2022 (print)
LCC HM736 (ebook) | DDC 302.34–dc23
LC record available at https://lccn.loc.gov/2020056039
LC ebook record available at https://lccn.loc.gov/2020056040

Editor: Eliza Leahy
Designer: Molly Ballanger

Photo Credits: kali9/iStock, cover; Quickly Fy/Shutterstock, 1; pikselstock/Shutterstock, 3l; Ovsianka/Shutterstock, 3r; Amorn Suriyan/iStock, 4; Ilnaz Bagautdinov/Shutterstock, 5 (background); Atstock Productions/Shutterstock, 5 (foreground); Laugesen Mateo/Shutterstock, 6l; PRASANNAPIX/Shutterstock, 6r; Geri Lavrov/Getty, 7; FREELY ART/Shutterstock, 8–9; Iakov Filimonov/Shutterstock, 10–11; all_about_people/Shutterstock, 12–13; MPH Photos/Shutterstock, 14–15; Wavebreakmedia/iStock, 16–17; ranplett/iStock, 18; Darrin Henry/Shutterstock, 19; Courtney Hale/iStock, 20–21.

Printed in the United States of America at Corporate Graphics in North Mankato, Minnesota.